Introduction

A Brief History of the S Class

Locomotive 171 *Slieve Gullion* first saw the light of day at the works of Beyer Peacock in Manchester in 1913. All five locomotives of the S class were delivered in February of that year to the North Wall in Dublin. From there they were hauled to Dundalk to be fully erected and tested.

The design work was done under the direction of Charles Clifford but much of the design is probably down to L. J. Watson, the Chief Draughtsman. Clifford retired just as the locomotives were being ordered and the new Locomotive Engineer, George T. Glover, made some small changes.

The new locomotives were 170 *Errigal*, 171 *Slieve Gullion*, 172 *Slieve Donard*, 173 *Galteemore* and 174 *Carrantuohill*. They were the first Great Northern locomotives to carry the nameplates on the driving wheel splasher rather than on the front ring of the boiler. They went to work on the increasingly heavy Dublin-Belfast passenger trains and were an immediate success.

The five S class locomotives were followed in 1915 by three locomotives of the closely-related S2 class. The new locomotives were to be named and the plates were cast but it seems unlikely that they were fitted or at least not for very long. No. 190 was to be *Lugnaquilla*, 191 *Carlingford* and 192 *Mounthamilton*. This last one is a bit of a puzzler. I am now convinced that the name does not come from a mountain at all but from the name of the Locomotive Engineer's house and the townland in which Dundalk station is built!

The Ss lost their nameplates about 1923 though 170 managed to retain hers until May 1930. At the same time the Brunswick Green livery gave way to the unrelieved black of the S2 locomotives.

In June 1926, *Slieve Donard* got an S2 boiler with a pressure of 200 pounds per square inch. This brought about a 10% reduction in coal used and the other locomotives were similarly treated but instead of getting new boilers, they got new fireboxes only. No. 171 was dealt with in December 1926 when the length of valve travel was increased from $3^3/4$ to $4^{25}/_{32}$ of an inch. This was so successful that the others got the same treatment by August 1928.

In 1932, railways all over these islands were making great accelerations and the Great Northern naturally turned to the new Compounds to work to the faster times. To the surprise of very few, it was soon found that the S class were well able for the new timings with a load of 7 or 8 bogies.

In August 1935, the Great Northern sent 170 to York Road in an exchange with their 2-6-0 No. 96 *Silver Jubilee* which had its nameplates boarded over for the visit. No. 96 worked between Belfast and Dublin. No. 170 worked round trips from Belfast to Portrush and Larne Harbour each day. While 96 was economical on coal, 170 impressed the NCC with her low water consumption.

Then in March 1936, locomotive 172 was fitted for oil burning and 171 *Slieve Gullion* was similarly converted that July. Both reverted to coal burning the following December.

In 1937 it was decided that the 25-year old S class locomotives should be renewed. By now Glover had been succeeded by George B. Howden who delegated locomotive responsibility to H. R. McIntosh. McIntosh became Locomotive Superintendent when Howden was made General Manager in 1939.

Although described as rebuilds or renewals, the locomotives were almost totally new and were allocated new building numbers by Dundalk Works. No dimensions changed although the new locomotives were heavier. No. 173 was the first of the new locomotives to appear in May 1938 (Works No. 40) and 192 followed in June (Works No 41). *Slieve Gullion* (Works No 42) left the Works in September 1938 and 172 (No 43) the following month. In June 1939, 191 emerged (Works No 44), followed by 170 (45) in June and 190 (46) the next month. 174 brought up the tail in October 1939 (No 47). The original names were restored to the S class locomotives and the S2s got names for the first time — 190 was *Lugnaquilla*, as intended before, but 191 was now *Croagh Patrick* and 192 *Slievenamon*. While most of the nameplates were like the S class plates of 1913, 190 carried the resurrected 1915 plates . It had the same cut-out and surrounding line of black wax as the preserved *Mounthamilton* plate referred to in the captions. All of the locomotives now had the lined blue livery introduced a few years earlier on the Compounds.

Most of the new locomotives now had D1 tenders holding 3500 gallons of water and 6 tons of coal, the same as 171's current tender. Some retained the shorter 2500 gallon B4 tenders (seen in the *Railway Magazine* plate) with flared tops so that they could turn at Warrenpoint. In 1946 Nos. 171-173 had these.

The new S and S2 locomotives did as much main line work as the Compounds, if not more. The late Bob Clements commented that the Ss were now doing harder work than any 4-4-0 of comparable size and probably doing as much as the LNER (ex - Great Central) *Directors* which were much larger.

At that time, international rugby matches were played at Ravenhill in Belfast and Fred Graham recalls seeing all 5 Ss leaving Adelaide coupled together to go down the Third Line to Great Victoria Street to work the return excursions. What a sight that must have been!

For some time in 1939 and all through 1940, *Slieve Donard* was again fitted for oil burning and again between September 1945 and August 1946.

From 1942, the Ss began to appear on the Derry Road — from Portadown to Londonderry (Foyle Road). For this, the tenders were equipped with the GNR's pattern of staff net — indeed 171's tender retains the slots needed to extend and retract this unwieldy looking device. The Ss were less well liked than the older Q class whose shorter wheel base and lighter frames allowed them to take the Derry Road's banks and curves much better.

No. 191 worked a 7-bogie trial train before the introduction of the *Enterprise* and had no trouble keeping a $2\frac{1}{4}$hour non-stop timing. A Compound worked the inaugural train but an S class with 6 or 7 bogies was soon the norm. After a few months, however, the three-cylinder simple VS class locomotives appeared and took over. This left little Dublin-Belfast work for the S class though they continued to be used on the Derry Road, Warrenpoint and, less frequently, Cavan trains.

In 1949, Nos. 173 and 192 got a new type of Davies exhaust injector (see page 6) and shortly afterwards, *Errigal* and *Slieve Gullion* were both fitted with a live steam injector, made in Dundalk by Paddy Mallon. It was designed to be serviced without dismantling. No. 171 retains this fitting on the fire-man's side, one of the very few injectors ever made in Ireland. It does not need retelling here that the GNR(I) was in deep financial trouble after the War and how, in 1953, its activities were vested in the Great Northern Railway (Board). Unlike the baby in the story of Solomon, the disputing parents killed off the child rather than agree on what to do with it. The result was that, in September 1958, the assets of the GNR(B) were formally divided between the Ulster Transport Authority and Córas Iompair Éireann the nationalised transport bodies in Northern Ireland and the Republic of Ireland respectively.

Locomotives 170, 171, 174 and 191 went to CIE while 172, 173, 190 and 192 went to the UTA who renumbered them 60, 61, 62, and 63 in that order.

On CIE, 191 was condemned in February 1960 but the other three locomotives fared better. No. 170 had been shopped at Dundalk in 1959 and both *Slieve Gullion* and *Carrantuohill* were shopped in 1960. All three were given new lined blue paintwork but 174 got the full treatment of lettering and crests in June 1960, when she was the last locomotive to leave Dundalk Works.

On the UTA, most of the locomotives were eventually put through the works at York Road. No. 62 appeared in UTA black lined red and straw, in April 1961. The sunken wax letters in the nameplates were now painted red. No. 63 was similarly treated in June 1961, and *Slieve Donard* the following November. *Galteemore* had been renumbered 61 but did not get another shopping.

The UTA seemed intent on getting rid of its railways but various legal battles delayed the inevitable closures. By early 1963, locomotive maintenance had fallen below the point of no return for many locomotives and new wheels were needed if the service was to be run at all. The answer lay in the purchase of four redundant locomotives from CIE which had finished with steam in April 1963. In June of that year, locomotives 170, 171, 174 and VS class 4-4-0 207 *Boyne* were sold to the UTA. All four lost their brass nameplates before the sale — one of 171's plates is now in the County Museum at Armagh.

On Apprentice Boys' day, 10th August 1963, *Errigal* worked a special from Belfast to Londonderry (Foyle Road) and the 10.35am back to Belfast, the 3.00pm Derry and a 7.30pm special back to Belfast! Both *Slieve Gullion* and *Carrantuohill* were in action on the Derry Road that day too, but on less intensive rosters.

Locomotive 61 slipped away at an auction on 20th March 1964, still wearing the battered blue livery. But there was a high day on 23rd May when a Sunday School excursion organised by Fred Graham brought 171 and 174 to Portrush. On the other hand 62 was stopped in July of that year.

On 3rd January 1965 the axe fell on the Warrenpoint branch and on 14th February the Derry Road was closed. At the same time all UTA goods trains disappeared leaving only the cross-border trains to Belfast and Derry (Waterside) running. Workings continued on the GNR Derry Road for some weeks, clearing wagons and stripping assets for shipment to Portadown's goods store. *Slieve Donard* was the last locomotive out of Derry and eventually arrived in Portadown with her smokebox adorned with forlorn slogans such as "We will rise again".

Slieve Gullion survived. It was the subject of a preservation attempt by the newly-formed Railway Preservation Society of Ireland which had set the preservation of an S class locomotive as its first priority. No. 171 remained in store at Adelaide shed and was leased to the Society by the Northern Ireland Transport Holding Company from 1st January 1966. She remained at Adelaide until 14th May 1966, when she was again in steam and hauled an ex-BCDR horsebox, an open wagon, an Inglis bread truck and J15 class 0-6-0 No. 186 (doubling as a brake van) to store in Ballymena shed.

By the end of the year, 171 was brought to York Road (Belfast) and stored in the open at what had been an access line to the nearby Duncrue Street Works. While waiting for a boiler test and a decision on how to have her overhauled, she worked one railtour to Larne Harbour. Afterwards she resumed her position in the open but lost several brass cab fittings in two raids. Fortunately the UTA was able to supply replacements.

At this time, the RPSI Committee was exploring the possibility of having the locomotive overhauled in Dundalk but it had lost too many of its heavy facilities and skills by then. In the end, the locomotive went to Harland and Wolff's shipyard on 12th April 1968 where, amongst other things, they straightened the frames which had a preference for going round right-hand bends! *Slieve Gullion* was brought by road to York Road goods yard on 28th July 1968 and was hauled to the shed yard by ex-SLNCR 0-6-4T No. 27 *Lough Erne*.

The locomotive was now paired with a 4000 gallon VS tender, GNR No. 31, which had come north with 207 *Boyne* in June 1963. This tender, however, has a Beyer Peacock maker's plate number 6964 linking it to one of *Boyne*'s sisters, 209 *Foyle*, which had gone for scrap with a 3500 gallon tender. When the time came for 207's demise at Adelaide, an escape committee of enthusiasts and helpful shed staff ensured that the tender did not follow 207 on her final journey.

After sitting in York Road locomotive yard for some months, *Slieve Gullion* spent two weeks as York Road station pilot before running to Lisburn goods store on 27th January 1969. There, volunteers applied five coats of blue paint generously supplied by Courtneys. Incidentally, 171 shared the shed with a tenderless *Merlin* which was in store waiting for a move to Belfast Transport Museum (Witham Street).

No. 171 returned to York Road in March 1969 and was again used to shunt the passenger station. At that time too, she worked a train of sleepers to Cullybackey and, on 3rd April, brought the 36 ton steam crane and its entourage to Knockmore Junction where a non-fitted Derry goods had been derailed.

Then on Easter Tuesday, 8th April, *Slieve Gullion* worked the 10.25am scheduled service to Portrush. Unfortunately the locomotive had two hot boxes on arrival and did nothing further that day. After re-weighing and checking the lubrication, she successfully worked a six-coach trial to Coleraine and back on 17th April. All was now set for 171 to take part in the RPSI's second two-day tour, the ambitious *Brian Boru* to Cork and Cobh. The lining was completed, crests applied and new replica nameplates fitted.

After a splendid run from Belfast on the Saturday morning of the tour, 171 blew a cylinder gland at Castlebellingham and every fourth beat of the exhaust produced a loud explosion of lost steam. *Slieve Gullion* followed 2-6-4T No. 4 to Cork and worked an evening trip to Cobh and back. The staccato exhaust echoing across the mudflats of Lough Mahon in the gathering gloom had an eerie quality.

Thus began 171's tour operations which I do not propose to detail here. They have been handsomely chronicled in Joe Cassells' excellent *Steam's Silver Lining* (1990) which is required reading!

I very much hope that you enjoy what follows.

The S class as built   This is the frontispiece from the September 1913 *Railway Magazine* — reproduced by kind permission of the Editor. No. 174 Carrantuohill is shown here as built and in its original Brunswick green livery. Indeed it is in its very earliest condition, for the casing at the base of the Ramsbottom safety valves was soon to be painted vermillion. Note the sand pipes for each driving wheel and the sandbox operating rod emerging from behind the front of the leading splasher. The brake rigging sits outside the wheels and there are splashers over the bogie wheels. The locomotive has an exhaust injector which is the grey pipe emerging from the back of the smokebox. As built, the S class were fitted with 2500 gallon B4 tenders, flared out at the top to increase coal capacity.

Dundalk running shed in 1956 The renewed No. 172 *Slieve Donard* emerged from Dundalk Works in October 1938 and is seen here when coupled to a Compound's 3500 gallon tender. The main visible differences from 174 in the previous picture are that the frames are deeper, the brake rigging is now behind the wheels and only the leading driving wheels have sanding gear which is now steam-operated. The cabsides now sport small vertical windscreens, the safety valves are Ross Pop pattern and, of course, the livery is lined blue. Between 1915 and 1938 the S class had been painted in the standard GNR black livery. Note the newly-shopped open wagons in the background with the long wagon-building shop behind them. The main line is beyond the wagon shop. After the Works closed, the wagon-building shop became a maintenance garage for the CIE road buses.

D Cobbe/Author's collection.

Adelaide Shed, Belfast, in 1952 No. 192 *Slievenamon* is an S2 class locomotive. Delivered from Beyer Peacock on 3rd March 1915, she was to have been named *Mounthamilton*. Although the plates were cast they were probably never used though one plate survives in the collection of the Irish Railway Record Society (see IRRS Journal Vol 9 p272). The locomotive was 'renewed' at Dundalk in June 1938 when she was named *Slievenamon* and received the blue livery. Here 192 has an exhaust injector on the right, or fireman's, side and you can see its steam pipe making its way from the back of the smokebox and along the top of the framing before disappearing past the crankaxle to somehow or other reappear between the driving wheels — but out of range of the coupling rod. Just what plumbing and fitting skills this called for are probably best left unexplored! The light has caught the two grey-looking door stops on the smokebox door hinges. These were fitted after a fatal accident on the LNER, when a smokebox door, which had been opened through 180°, was blown shut, killing a fireman. These stops limited the opening to just 90°. No. 171 retains these stops.

Colour-Rail

Great Victoria Street, Belfast, on 1st September 1964 The last summer timetable for the Derry Road and the Warrenpoint branch had only a few days to run when this scene was captured. Here we see 170 *Errigal* setting out from Platform 3 with the 3.00pm to Londonderry (Foyle Road) while 2-6-4T No. 55 takes water before working the 3.15pm to Dublin. No. 170's train has an O1 class former slip carriage N236 (a brake composite) marshalled next to the locomotive — note the distinctive end windows. Above the tank engine rises the distinctive tower of the Presbyterian Assembly Buildings, built in 1905 on the site of Fisherwick Presbyterian Church at a time when most of the congregation had moved away to the Malone Road area. The crown steeple was considered to be 'suitably Scottish' and it has remained a landmark ever since. There is a glimpse of the green dome of the City Hall on the extreme right. No. 170 is actually in blue livery and it is hard to recall that the locomotives really were this dirty! A hint of blue is just visible round the engine number on the cab side.

J D FitzGerald

7

Portadown on 11th September 1965 This was the Railway Preservation Society Ireland's inaugural railtour. Initially hauled by ex-GNR UG class 0-6-0 No. 49 (formerly GNR No. 149), the tour went from York Road to Portrush and then to Lisburn. It was this tour that introduced runpasts to the United Kingdom (from Canada, I seem to recall?) and there were three on the Antrim branch. *Slieve Gullion* was scheduled to work the train from Lisburn to Portadown and back to Great Victoria Street but some members privately funded the addition of 207 *Boyne* as a last minute surprise. This turned out to be *Boyne*'s last run. Here the train has arrived, unusually, at Platform 3 and the locomotives are about to go to Portadown shed for turning — the last time that Portadown turntable was used. The coach next to No. 207 is No. 180, a C2 First Class coach which had been experimentally painted red earlier in the year. On arrival back in Belfast, 171's whistle stuck open and was only silenced after the application of several spanners and a large hammer! The superstitious among us took this to be a good omen!

J D FitzGerald

Larne Harbour on 8th October 1966 Railway Preservation Society of Ireland members had put in a lot of hard work into having her as blue as possible for this trip, her only one in preservation before entering Harland and Wolff's for overhaul. It was, incidentally, the first time that a Society-owned locomotive worked on a public railway in the UK. Here, 171 waits below the upper quadrant signals of Larne Harbour before the return to York Road. Upper quadrant signals are rare in Ireland. The driver, the late Davy McDonald (just visible as the rear figure at the cab steps), later described the locomotive as "very lively indeed". The second and fourth vehicles on the train are two of the famous North Atlantic Express coaches built for the NCC in 1934-35. The five vehicles of this set had five foot wide windows, at a time when the standard of the parent LMS company was four foot six inches. The late Sam Carse, long-time RPSI Dublin Agent and Mr Fix-it for steam on CIE, is the man looking left in the right foreground.

J D FitzGerald

Left: **The Wheeldrop** This was built in 1977-78, mostly by Society members, to eliminate a lot of difficult jacking. Here 171, the first customer, has her leading driving wheels supported on a pair of beams connected to winches at the top of the gantry. With the sections of running rail removed, the wheelset can be lowered into the pit from which it can be removed without moving the locomotive. Here, 171 is attended by Brian Hill and Johnny Glendinning with John Friel in the pit while Peter Scott is largely hidden as he checks on progress. Note the oval steel plate on the valance commemorating the Harland and Wolff overhaul; it has since been replaced.

Right: **The Wheel Lathe** Once out of the wheeldrop pit, a wheelset is placed in the adjacent wheel lathe. This massive machine, dating from 1924, came from the works at York Road. Here a journal on 171's crank axle is receiving attention in April 1986 , before a newly-cast brass axlebox is fitted. Remember, the wheels are 6' 7" inches in diameter; note too how massive the big ends are.

Left: **Frames** In late 1989, 171's boiler was removed from the frames for the first time in preservation for a heavy rebuild. This unusual view, looking forward from the cab area, shows what is sometimes called the "bottom half" of a locomotive. On the extreme left and right are the driving wheel splashers. The pipes sticking up at the far end of the locomotive are main steam pipes that bring the steam from the superheater to the piston valves and pistons. The covers of the two piston valves are visible below each steam pipe.

Ballykelly on 17th October 1970 The Society's Colmcille Tour brought 171 *Slieve Gullion* and five NIR bogies to Londonderry (Waterside) and the train is seen here en route to the Maiden City. The runway here had to be extended across the NCC main line during the last war to accommodate Liberators and other heavy aircraft. This called for the signalling to be interlocked with the flight control tower. After the war, the airfield continued to be used by RAF Coastal Command who flew Shackletons far into the Atlantic, mostly on maritime reconnaissance and submarine monitoring as well as weather observation duties. The airfield commander provided an escort of RAF Military Police (see the gent in the white belt), a fire tender to add some colour, and a Mark 2 Shackleton, its Rolls Royce Griffon engines roaring, as a fine backdrop! No. 171 here has the 4000-gallon VS class tender which she had from the time she left Harland and Wolff's until 1973. Once again the set contains two North Atlantic coaches, but by now they are repainted in NIR's "excursion only" livery of maroon with a broad grey stripe along the waist. One of these two, the third vehicle in the train, is No. 472, now preserved as LMS NCC No. 91.

Larne Harbour on 28th April 1973 During the Colmcille Tour, 171 suffered a hot left big end and a blown right-hand piston gland. At this time, all available RPSI funds were being diverted into the 2-6-4T fund and all manpower into building a 3-road extension to the existing red-brick locomotive shed at Whitehead. In the winter of 1972-73 though, things picked up. No. 171's driving boxes were remetalled at Harland and Wolff's and the small 3500 gallon tender from her CIE and UTA days (GNR No. 12) was renovated. A repaint of the locomotive pro-duced this light shade of blue, as yet unlined. At that time, the Society advertised its running-in trips under the brand name of *King Fergus* and here the first of them shunts at Larne Harbour under the upper quadrant signals. The train includes what was in 1973 the entire carriage stock of the RPSI — the unrestored Great Northern Directors' Saloon No. 50, and the ex-Great Southern and Western Railway Rosslare First/Second/Brake No. 861. The locomotive headlamps are GSWR pattern and sit rather high on 171's GNR brackets.

Portrush on 2nd August 1975 The RPSI ran its first *Portrush Flyer* on 28th July 1973 when the adult fare was £1.40. Under 14's travelled for 90p and a whole carriage for the day cost £60. The train takes its name from a pre-war NCC express . The *Portrush Flyer* continues the long Ulster tradition of travelling behind steam to spend a Saturday at the seaside. It is now the longest-established public steam excursion in these islands if not in Europe or even further afield! The *Flyers* were usually the pre-serve of 2.6.4T No. 4 as 171 *Slieve Gullion* had unfortunate experiences on earlier runs to Portrush.

However, all is well in this evening shot at Portrush as 171 pre-pares for the homeward run to York Road and Whitehead. Earlier she had been to Londonderry, light engine, to turn. The red-on-white headboard lasted until the summer of 1984 when it gave way to one with raised brass letters on a red ground. The first coach is ex-GNR K15 Open Third No. 583 which had come into RPSI ownership. The varying liveries on the seven bogie train reflects the diverse origins of the early RPSI carriage fleet.

The siding on the left has since been lifted.

Dromin Junction on 4th October 1975 This day saw the last steam train from Belfast Great Victoria Street and the last on the Ardee branch. Here 171 brings the train off the branch to rejoin the Great Northern main line and continue south to Drogheda. Time was lost while shunting at Ardee and the stop at Dromin Junction had to be cut out to avoid excessive late running. Dromin has here lost its footbridge and the loop and siding alongside the branch platform, but the island platform retains the waiting room — 42 years after the branch lost its passenger traffic and 20 years after the main line trains had stopped calling! The branch saw its last trains on 1st November 1975 and the cabin finally closed on 17th January 1976. The train, like that on page 13, is a mixture of NIR, CIE and RPSI liveries. The red livery seen on three of the vehicles is similar to that used in the 1930s by both the LMS NCC and the Great Southern Railway of Ireland. Note the damaged platform beside 171 — this dates from a railcar derailment here on 12th December 1969.

Londonderry (Waterside) on 3rd September 1977 A long distance running-in trip for 171, (following more axlebox work) waits at the Maiden City for its return working. The train has four carriages but NIR vans at the buffers make it seem longer. As in the earlier picture at Portrush, the carriage next to the locomotive is ex-GNR(I) K15 Open Third No. 583. This vehicle was fully restored at Whitehead, had its wheels reprofiled on the underfloor lathe at Inchicore and was repainted at Mullingar. It was totally destroyed in a malicious fire at Whitehead in March 1978. Londonderry once had four termini, one narrow gauge and one standard gauge on each bank of the Foyle. Waterside is the only surviving terminus, though replaced in 1980 by the present NIR station, built beyond the terminal building seen here, and closer to Craigavon Bridge and the city centre. The clock tower visible here, built in 1878, still survives as part of the original station which today serves as a seldom used goods depot.

FitzGerald Platform on 17th May 1980 Reflecting the confidence she now enjoyed, *Slieve Gullion* worked the vast bulk of the *South Kerry* tour single-handed. J15 0-6-0 No. 184 worked boat train connections to and from Dublin (Connolly) but the rest of the mileage was all down to 171 and she reeled off the miles to Tralee on the Saturday in fine style. She is seen here in the late afternoon of a splendid day when the weather was almost too good — endless cloudless skies and very warm. This is about a mile west of Killarney, climbing at 1 in 100 past the overgrown and disused halt built to serve a nearby Gaelic Athletic Association sportsground. In the warm air, the sharp exhaust has evaporated very quickly leaving an uninterrupted view across the valley of the River Flesk to the Mangerton Mountains. The train is by now in uniform livery despite the varying coach profiles. The first and fourth carriages are of GNR origin, the third is NCC and the remainder Great Southern. The leading coach, Brake First 231 (GNR class D5), retains the heavy rubber corridor connection from its BUT railcar days. This is the only slide in this book to have been published before, in the Jarrold's Railway World Calendar for 1982.

Lisburn on 31st August 1981 The RPSI ran its first public excursions to Dublin, under the title *Steam Enterprise* on 20th September 1980 and two further trips were planned for September 1981. The stock was stabled at Bangor while the locomotive and workshop coach set up camp in the Central Service Depot at Belfast. As a result, the trains started from Bangor. Here the empty stock (far from empty!) is working its way to Bangor and approaches Lisburn off the third line from Knockmore and Antrim. It is framed by a remarkable gantry of semaphore signals, which was installed when Lisburn was remodelled and resignalled in 1977. This was probably the last such construction in Europe (if not the world!) apart from preserved lines. Counting the semaphore arms visible in the picture is quite an exercise — you should find 20. Lisburn is now all electric. The goods store, behind the locomotive, has given way to a modern office block. The water column, beyond the left leg of the gantry, is still operational. The leading carriage is again ex-GSWR Brake Composite No. 861 of 1906.

Cloghogue Chapel on 19th September 1981 Here 171 *Slieve Gullion* has the last of the Bangor to Dublin trains near the top of the 8½ mile Wellington Bank, most of which is at gradients between 1 in 113 and 1 in 100. For no less than 43 years in the last century, the Parish Priest here was a Father Michael Murphy and he gave his name to the bridge over the Dublin Road (about the rear of the train above). The Roman Catholic church on the right, in the townland of Cloghogue (pronounced Clog), has been a landmark for engine crews ever since its opening at Easter 1916. Indeed reaching here with a difficult southbound train was often quite a relief. Although properly known as the Church of the Sacred Heart and built during the time of Canon McNally, who was also 43 years in the Parish, railwaymen credited the new building to the long-departed Father Murphy. It has even been called "Father Murphy's Orange Hall". Photography here was impossible for some years due to the proximity of military installations on the Dublin-Belfast road. With the ceasefire in Northern Ireland, times are changing and perhaps such photographs will soon be possible again.

Limerick shed on 16th May 1982 The *Thomond Railtour* of the weekend of May 14th-16th brought 171 and J15 0-6-0 No. 184 to an overnight stop in Limerick. While 184 worked to Foynes and back on the Sunday morning, 171 was prepared at Limerick shed and she is seen here sitting alongside the foreman's office, outside the former Waterford, Limerick and Western Railway's works and its superbly arched doorway. Note the oil feeder on the running plate and spilled sand on the ground below where the sandboxes have been topped up with dry sand. No. 171's intermittent hot driving box problem had recently been traced to a defective ratchet spindle in the mechanical lubricator on the other side of the locomotive's frames.

The preserved *Slieve Gullion* has now travelled over most parts of the Irish railway system. She has yet to work west of Claremorris or south from there to Limerick and on to Foynes. She has not yet covered the Carrick-on-Suir to Waterford line and, curiously, has not been to either Howth or Barrack Street (Dundalk) since preservation. Apart from that, she has been just about everywhere!

Knockmore Junction on 14th May 1984 This was a year of celebration for the Railway Preservation Society of Ireland, because it won the highly coveted annual award of the Association of Railway Preservation Societies. The 1984 two-day tour to Galway finished at Belfast Central on the Sunday night. The empty stock working to Whitehead on the Monday was, and remains, a most relaxed affair with the pleasant mixture of main line running, a fairly empty train and little of the hyper pressure of the previous two days. Knockmore Junction cabin closed on 28th May 1977 when the third line was opened between here and Lisburn. Here *Slieve Gullion* slows for the curve onto the branch proper as she heads the nominally empty train on the long trek for home. In those days, of course, Belfast Central to Whitehead was 68 route miles and two reversals away, rather than the present 17 mile saunter. As an experiment in 1984, the train worked beyond Whitehead to give a boat connection at Larne Harbour and this proved to be so popular that it has featured as the final leg of many of the big tours ever since. The second, fourth and last vehicles of this train are of NCC origin, the fourth being restored Dining Car No. 87 of 1950.

Kilbarry on 12th May 1985 This is a photograph that sums up much of what the RPSI is all about — main line steam as it was always meant to be. For the sixth successive year of big tours, 171 had the assistance of J15 No. 184 and here they tackle the climb out of Cork early on the Sunday morning. They have already battled up the 1 in 78 through the 1355-yard tunnel and then a stretch at 1 in 64. Just about here they have hit the start of two miles of 1 in 60 and the morning is cool enough for the condensing exhausts to hang long in the still air. In the background, the natural draught is still clearing the stour from the tunnel mouth. The train is passing Kilbarry cabin, here switched out. It closed on 29th March 1987 when the yard here finally closed. The right-hand of the two church towers belongs to Saint Peter and Paul's Roman Catholic Church while that on the left belongs to the Church of Ireland Church of St Anne, better known as the home of the Shandon Bells.

Magheramorne lagoon on 21st May 1988 Ever since seeing a classic William Robb photo in an old *Railway Magazine*, I had been trying to "crack" this location but getting the light and the steam together was always elusive. However, this day's *Carnival Coaster*, sponsored by Carrickfergus Borough Council, gave us another chance. No. 171 *Slieve Gullion* worked a round trip from York Road to Larne Harbour in connection with a medieval festival in Carrickfergus but there was nothing medieval about 171's performance. Right on cue, as 171 worked back to York Road, the clouds parted, the sun shone from the right place and the swan obligingly paddled into shot! Contrary to popular belief, the swan is real and not a clockwork decoy borrowed for the occasion! The locomotive was now sporting a deflector plate mounted between her safety valves. This is to allow her to work under the overhead wires of the DART (Dublin Area Rapid Transit) system, which opened in 1984.

Castlerock on 6th September 1991 The Northern Ireland Tourist Board commissioned an advertisement which was to include shots of 171 and train alongside the strand at Downhill. The day of filming was very overcast — in the shadow of the cliffs the light felt like the proverbial "fortnight at f4". The filming called for a camera platform on the side of the tender and lights on the coal. Nearly as drastic, Willie Graham and Mickey Hamill, the NIR crew, had their faces dirtied to make them look "more authentic". The train retreated to Castlerock to allow the regular Londonderry railcars to pass and, perversely, the sun came out. Fortunately, it stayed out long enough to capture this view of the train heading back to Downhill and passing Castlerock Church of Ireland. Beyond the church can be seen the wall of the Bar Mouth that brings the navigable River Bann far into the deep waters of the Atlantic. The Bar Mouth had its own steam locomotives during its construction. On the distant left the resort of Portstewart can be distinguished. The train sequence in the finished N.I. Tourist Board film, by the way, lasts about 8 seconds (out of 30).

Whitehead on 17th September 1994 A mirage of three Great Northern blue locomotives — enough to make a retired NIR Locomotive Inspector miss a heartbeat! On this day, 85 *Merlin* returned to traffic following extensive firebox repairs and went with 171 *Slieve Gullion* on the *Atlantic Coast Express* to Londonderry. The photograph was taken at 06.30 that morning and exposure was 3 seconds at f8. It shows the locomotives awaiting the arrival of the NIR crews. To the left is the new heavy lift area that is revolutionising carriage work and behind it is the carriage shed, partly funded by the International Fund for Ireland. The water tower and the red-brick shed were part of the Midland Railway (NCC) expansion of Whitehead around 1907. To the right of the red-brick shed is the three-road extension begun in 1971 and completed by Enterprise Ulster in 1978. 85 *Merlin* is here paired with her latest tender, GNR No. 73, built in 1948 by Beyer Peacock for U class 4-4-0 201 *Meath*. The top of the tender has been extensively rebuilt and remodelled to Compound profile. It now holds 3100 gallons of water compared to the original 2500. The VS 4000 gallon tender (No. 31) completes the picture by creating the illusion of a third blue engine! This tender can be seen paired with *Slieve Gullion* on page 11.